Contents

Parents' notes	2
1. Parts of a plant and their functions	4
2. Pollination	6
3. Healthy plants	8
4. Micro-organisms	10
5. Sorting and classifying	12
6. The seven life processes	14
TEST 1	16
7. Habitats and ecosystems	18
8. Food chains	20
9. Teeth	22
10. Muscles and bones	24
11. Nutrition	26
12. The heart and blood	28
TEST 2	30
13. Healthy living	32
14. Natural and synthetic materials	34
15. Solids, liquids and gases	36
16. Mixtures and filtration	38
17. Dissolving and evaporating	40
18. Sound	42
TEST 3	44
19. The Earth, the Sun and the Moon	46
20. Reversible and irreversible changes	48
21. Forces	50
22. Light and how we see things	52
23. Magnets	54
24. Electricity	56
TEST 4	58
Answers	60

Focus on Science

Year 5
age 9 to 10

Text and illustrations © Hodder Murray 2005

First published 2005
exclusively for WHSmith by
Hodder Murray,
a member of the Hodder Headline Group
338 Euston Road
London NW1 3BH

All rights reserved. Apart from any use permitted under UK copyright law, no part of this publication may be reproduced or transmitted in any form or by any means, electronic or mechanical, including photocopying, recording or any information storage and retrieval system, without permission in writing from the publisher.

Impression number   10 9 8 7 6 5 4 3 2
Year   2010 2009 2008 2007 2006 2005

Text: Lynn Huggins-Cooper

Typeset by Servis Filmsetting Ltd, Manchester

Printed and bound in Spain

A CIP record for this book is available from the British Library

ISBN 0 340 88769 9

Parents' notes

How this book can help your child

- This book has been written for children who are between 9 and 10 years old.
- It will support and improve the work they are doing at school, whichever science course they use.
- The activities in the book have been carefully written to include the knowledge expected of children at this stage in their development.
- The book offers support, development and challenge for all abilities.
- Working through the activities will help to reinforce work carried out at school and will help your child to approach tests with confidence.

Using the book

- There are 24 topics and 4 tests in the book. A test occurs after 6 topics have been completed.
- Each topic need not be completed in one session. Think of it as about a week's work.
- Try to supplement "paper" activities with safe, hands-on science activities: use cooking as an opportunity to look at changes of state and reversible/irreversible change; spend time in the garden or the park, looking at plant and animal diversity, etc.
- Do give help and encouragement. Completing the activities should not become a chore. Remember your child has already spent a whole tiring day at school!
- Do leave out a specific topic until later should your child not have covered its content in school. The book has been written to support the teaching in school, not to pre-empt it.
- Do let your child mark his or her own work under your supervision and correct any careless mistakes he or she might have made.
- When all the tests have been completed let your child fill in the Certificate of Achievement on the opposite page.
- Each double page has a title, explanation of the learning point, practice, extension and challenge.

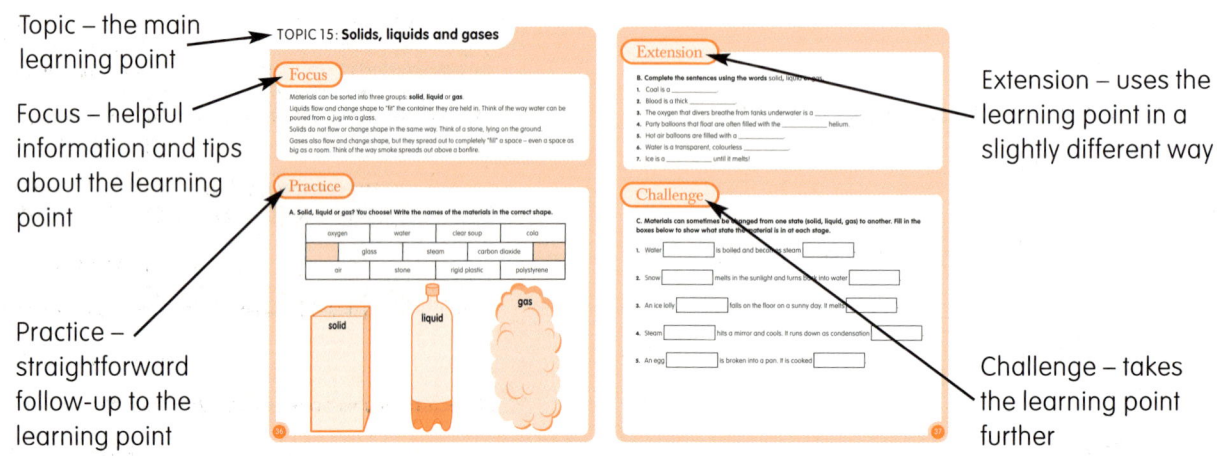

Topic – the main learning point

Focus – helpful information and tips about the learning point

Practice – straightforward follow-up to the learning point

Extension – uses the learning point in a slightly different way

Challenge – takes the learning point further

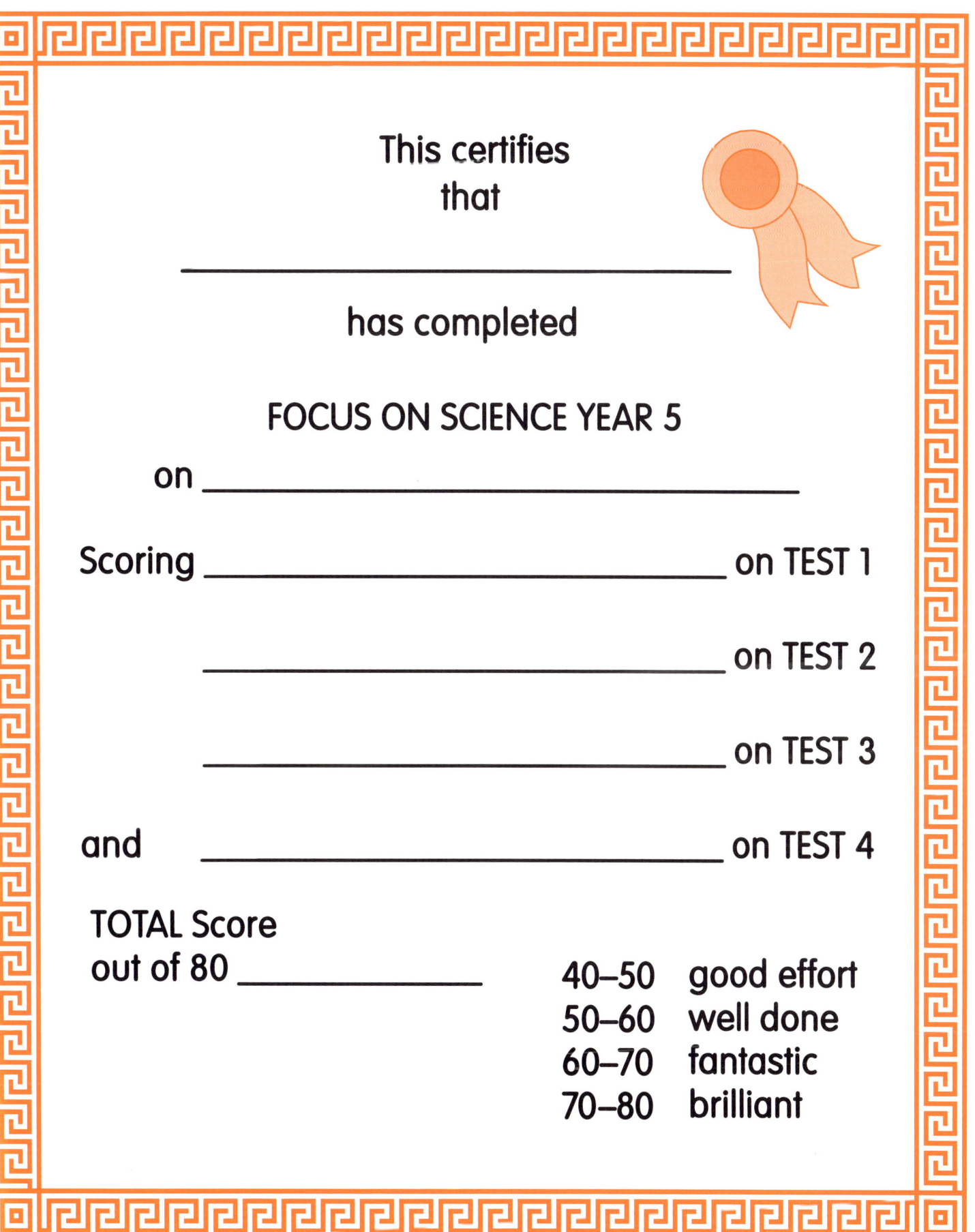

TOPIC 1: Parts of a plant and their functions

Focus

Each part of a plant has a different **function**.

Practice

A. Match the labels to the correct parts of this flowering plant.
Can you remember their function (job)? Write it below the label.

stem

root

leaf

petal

Extension

B. Match the descriptions to each part of the plant.

1. stem

2. root

3. leaf

4. petal

a. anchors the plant in the soil; takes up water and goodness from the soil

b. holds the flower up

c. makes food for the plant using sunlight

d. attracts insects with scent and colour

Challenge

C. Choose the best words to complete the sentences.

1. The root/leaf/stem helps to hold the plant steady in the soil.

2. When the plant is fertilised by pollen from another plant, leaves/roots/seeds will develop.

3. Leaves use energy from the shade/Sun/air to make food for the plant.

4. The stem helps to hold the flower up in the air, so that the wind or insects can carry the petals/pollen/plant to other plants for fertilisation to take place.

5. Green plants need light/dark/dry air to grow.

TOPIC 2: **Pollination**

Focus

Plants that are pollinated by insects often have large, bright petals and sweet nectar to attract the insects. Think of a lily or rose.

Plants that are pollinated by the wind have small petals and long **stamens** (the part of the plant that carries the pollen). These can wave in the wind and the pollen is blown a long way. A good example of a plant that is wind-pollinated is grass.

Practice

A. Look at the plants listed below. Do you think they are pollinated by the wind or by insects? Write wind **or** insect **in the boxes.**

1. grass

2. rose

3. buttercup

4. wheat

5. daisy

6. hazel catkins

7. violet

8. tulip

Extension

B. How do plants attract insects? Tick all the boxes you agree with.

1. by having brightly coloured petals .... ☐
2. by having long, wavy anthers to release pollen into the air .... ☐
3. by having scented flowers .... ☐
4. by having spiky leaves and spines .... ☐
5. by having sweet, sugary nectar .... ☐
6. by having long roots to anchor the plant in the soil .... ☐

Challenge

C. Design a flowering plant in the box. Add as many things as you can think of to attract insects to the plant.

Describe how your plant will attract insects. _____
_____
_____
_____

TOPIC 3: Healthy plants

Focus

Green plants need certain conditions so that they can grow properly. They need light, water and the correct temperature. Plants growing where there is not enough light are long and spindly and are often yellowy instead of green.

Practice

A. Tick the correct answers.

1. Which is the best place for a plant to grow?
    a. in a dark cupboard .... ☐
    b. under a bed, in the dark .... ☐
    c. on a bright, sunny windowsill .... ☐
    d. on a shady shelf .... ☐

2. Which answer describes a plant grown in the dark?
    a. yellowy leaves with a long, thin, floppy stem .... ☐
    b. green, juicy leaves with a stem that holds the plant up straight .... ☐

3. Which answer describes a plant grown without enough water?
    a. green, juicy leaves .... ☐
    b. floppy, brownish, crinkly leaves .... ☐

B. I am growing sunflowers for the garden. I planted the seeds and watered them. I have put them on a dark shelf on top of the radiator. Why is it not the best place for the plants to grow? Give TWO reasons.

_____
_____
_____
_____
_____

Extension

C. True or false? Put T **or** F **in the boxes.**

1. Plants need water and darkness to grow. ☐
2. Plants need light but not water to grow. ☐
3. Plants can turn blue if they are put in the dark. ☐
4. Plants can turn yellow if they are put in a dark place. ☐
5. Plants turn yellow because they need light to make their food. ☐
6. Plants can dry up if they have enough water but not enough light. ☐
7. Plants can quickly dry up if they are in a very warm place. ☐
8. If I take a yellowy plant from darkness and put it in a light place, it will gradually turn green again. ☐

Challenge

D. Match the descriptions to the correct plants.

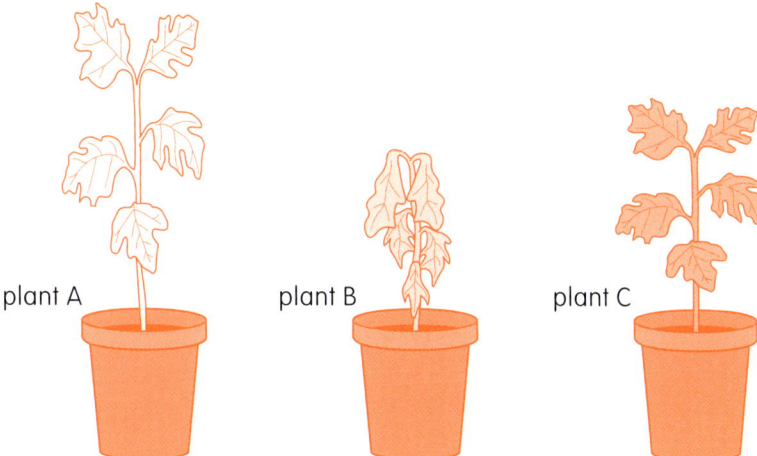

plant A   plant B   plant C

1. This plant has been grown on a windowsill. It has had plenty of light and water. This is plant _____.
2. This plant has been grown on a windowsill. It has had plenty of light but has not had enough water. This is plant _____.
3. This plant has been grown in a cupboard. It has been watered but has not had enough light. This is plant _____.

TOPIC 4: Micro-organisms

Focus

Micro-organisms are very small living things, such as bacteria, viruses or fungi. Some micro-organisms can be very dangerous and make people ill – but some can be very useful. Yoghurt and bread are both made using micro-organisms.

Practice

A. Fill in the missing words to complete the sentences.

| beer | yeast | rot | yoghurt | micro-organism | mouldy | viruses | bacteria |

1. Micro-organisms make bread go _____.

2. Micro-organisms are added to milk to make _____.

3. The bacteria that give us stomach upsets are a sort of _____.

4. Coughs and colds are caused by _____. They are a sort of micro-organism.

5. _____ found in the soil can make people ill. That is why we wash our hands after playing in the garden.

6. _____ is a drink made using a micro-organism.

7. Bread is made using _____.

8. Micro-organisms cause food to _____.

Extension

B. Match the correct beginning and ending to make sentences.

1. We keep milk in the fridge

2. Chicken pox

3. We cover food

4. We sneeze into a hankie

5. We wash our hands

a. to wash away bacteria and viruses.

b. to keep flies away. They carry micro-organisms that can make us sick.

c. so we do not spread viruses to other people.

d. to keep it cool. Bacteria grow and multiply more quickly in warm places.

e. is caused by a virus.

Challenge

C. Choose the correct words to complete the sentences.

| viruses | compost | bacteria | bread | sick |

1. Some micro-organisms are helpful, such as yeast. Yeast is used to make _____.

2. Yoghurt is made when special _____ are added to milk.

3. Bacteria help to break down _____ in the garden.

4. Bacteria can make people _____.

5. _____ make people ill. They cause illnesses such as flu and chicken pox.

TOPIC 5: Sorting and classifying

Focus

In science, sorting things into groups is called **classification**.

Plants and animals are sorted into groups according to the things they have in common. For example, birds and butterflies could be sorted into the same group because they both have wings.

Practice

A. Sort these animals into the correct part of the table.

| lion | whale | tadpole | dog | newt | shark | donkey |

lives in water	does not live in water

Extension

B. Sort these animals into two groups.

| alligator | whale | chicken | dog | penguin | python (snake) | donkey |

lays eggs	does not lay eggs

Challenge

C. This is a Venn diagram. Use it to sort the creatures into sets by drawing lines. Which creatures belong to both sets? They will go in the middle section to show they belong to both sets.

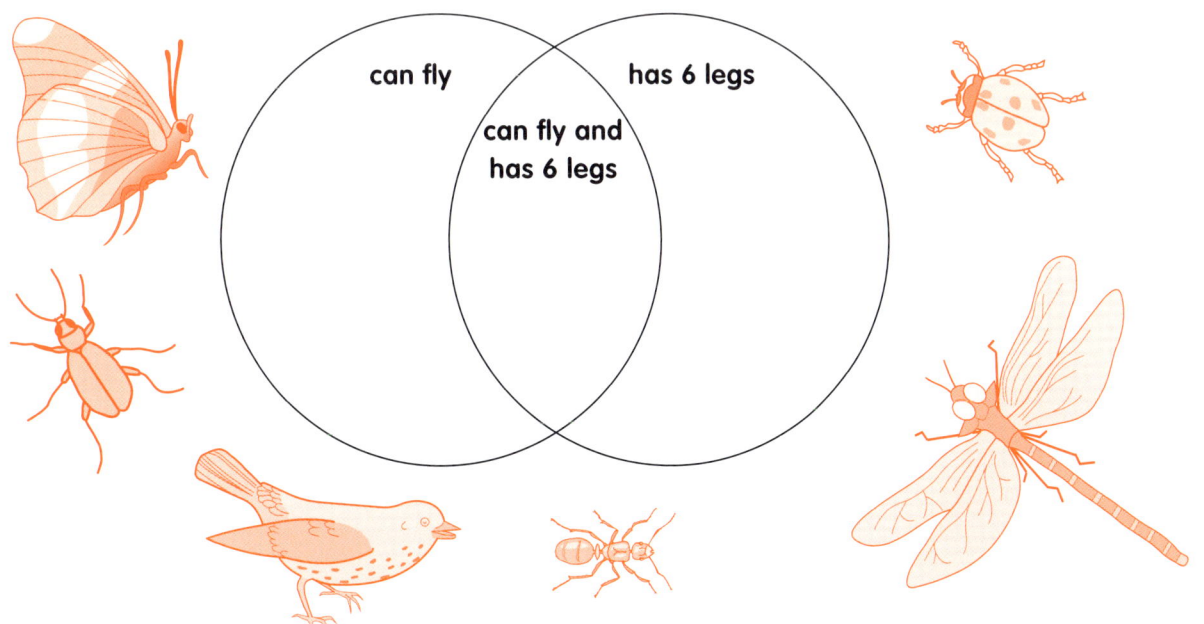

TOPIC 6: **The seven life processes**

Focus

All living things, both creatures and plants, do certain things – that is how we know they are alive!

All living things:
- move
- grow and change
- reproduce
- respire
- feel things
- feed
- get rid of waste.

Practice

A. Are these things alive or not alive? Put them into the correct part of the table.

| cat   spider   pebble   flames   water   sunshine   beetle |

alive	not alive

Extension

B. True or false? Put T or F in the boxes.

1. Cabbage plants are not really alive because they cannot walk about. ☐

2. Fire is alive because flames make a crackling noise. ☐

3. Water is alive because it moves. ☐

4. Giraffes are not alive although they move, feed and produce babies. ☐

5. Daisies are alive, even though we cannot see them moving about. ☐

6. All living things reproduce. ☐

Challenge

C. Imagine you are an alien. You have never seen fire or a mouse before. Put a tick or a cross in each of the boxes to decide whether each is alive or not alive.

	mouse	fire
Does it:		
move?	☐	☐
grow and change?	☐	☐
reproduce?	☐	☐
respire?	☐	☐
feel things?	☐	☐
feed?	☐	☐
get rid of waste?	☐	☐

TEST 1

Topic 1

1. **Match the part of the plant to its function.** (3 marks)

1. attracts insects with its scent and colour	a. leaf
2. anchors the plant in the ground	b. root
3. makes food using sunlight	c. petal

2. **Which part of a plant takes up water from the soil?** (1 mark) _____

3. **Why do green plants need sunlight?** (1 mark) _____
   _____

Topic 2

4. **Which features help plants to attract insects? Tick all the boxes you agree with.** (3 marks)

   a. brightly coloured petals............☐   d. spiky leaves and spines............☐
   b. long, wavy anthers to release   e. sweet, sugary nectar ....☐
      pollen into the air........................☐   f. long roots to anchor the plant
   c. scented flowers ....☐   in the soil ....☐

Topic 3

5. **What do plants need to grow?** (2 marks) _____
   _____

6. **What would happen to a plant that was not given enough water?** (1 mark) _____
   _____

7. **What would happen to a plant that did not have enough light?** (1 mark) _____
   _____

Topic 4

8. Why do we keep milk in the fridge? Explain your answer. (2 marks) _____
_____
_____

Topic 5

9. In science, what is meant by "classification"? (2 marks) _____
_____

Topic 6

10. Sort these things into the correct part of the table. (3 marks)

| sunshine   tadpole   plant growing in a pot   water   fire   oak tree |

alive	not alive

Mark the test. Remember to fill in your score on page 3.

Write your score out of 19. ☐

Add a BONUS POINT if you scored 15 or more.

TOTAL SCORE FOR TEST 1 ☐

How did you find the test?
Colour a face

too hard   too easy   about right

TOPIC 7: Habitats and ecosystems

Focus

A **habitat** is a place where certain types of plants and animals live. The seashore, the woods, the desert – they are all habitats. **Ecosystem** is the word used to describe a habitat and all the things (plants and animals) that live there.

Practice

A. Match the habitats to the plants and creatures that live there.

1. seashore	a. blackbird, snail, rose, ladybird
2. woodland	b. owl, badger, oak tree
3. garden	c. fox, dandelion, pigeon
4. town (urban)	d. crab, periwinkle, seaweed
5. rainforest	e. penguin, seal, killer whale
6. Antarctic	f. monkey, tree frog, orchid
7. desert	g. camel, scorpion, snake

Extension

B. Fill in the missing words in the sentences below.

| habitat | woodland | seashore | ladybirds | desert |

1. A _____ is the name given to a place where a collection of plants and animals live.

2. The _____ is the name given to the habitat where we would find crabs and sea anemones.

3. _____ is a type of habitat that contains trees, and possibly owls and badgers.

4. The _____ is the name given to the habitat where we could find cacti and camels.

5. A garden habitat could contain trees, flowering plants, foxes and _____.

Challenge

C. Answer these.

1. Name three animals you could find in a woodland habitat.
   _____   _____   _____

2. Name three animals or plants you could find in a rainforest habitat.
   _____   _____   _____

3. Name three animals you could find on the seashore.
   _____   _____   _____

4. Name a plant and an animal you could find in a desert.
   _____   _____

5. What is a habitat?
   _____
   _____

TOPIC 8: Food chains

Focus

Food chains are collections of plants and animals, written in order in a chain because they eat one another. An example would be:

lettuce ⟶ slug ⟶ bird

The chains really start with the Sun, because green plants get their energy from the Sun. The energy from the Sun helps them to grow. They are eaten by animals, which are in turn eaten by other animals.

Practice

A. Put these food chains in the correct order.

1. seaweed   otter   fish

2. snail   cabbage   hedgehog

3. fox   grass   rabbit

4. plant   robin   caterpillar

5. owl   nuts   mouse

Extension

B. Who am I? Choose the correct animal or plant from the box below.

| caterpillar   seagull   hedgehog   rabbit   lettuce |

1. I eat plants. I am eaten by birds. I am a _____.
2. I eat slugs and snails. I am sometimes eaten by foxes. I am a _____.
3. I am eaten by slugs and snails. I am a _____.
4. I eat fish. I am a _____.
5. I eat plants. I am eaten by foxes. I am a _____.

Challenge

C. Use the plants and creatures in the word wall below to draw the food chains for each habitat.

	cabbage	pondweed	fish	
seeds	mouse	thrush	owl	
	slug	dragonfly larva		

1. Garden food chain

2. Woodland food chain

3. Pond food chain

TOPIC 9: Teeth

Focus

Teeth are for tearing and chewing food. Different types of animals, with different diets, need different types of teeth.

Animals who do not eat meat need teeth designed for grinding tough plants such as grass and leaves. Animals who only eat meat need teeth for killing prey and tearing chunks of meat. Humans need a mixture of both types of teeth as we usually have a mixed diet of meat and vegetables.

Our teeth help us to chew our food into small pieces, so that our digestive systems can break the food down. Then our bodies are able to use the goodness in the foods, such as vitamins.

We should clean our teeth in the morning and before we go to bed to get rid of any bits of food left behind after we eat. The bacteria in our mouths break food down into sugars that make **plaque**. Plaque is sticky and coats our teeth. If we do not brush it away, it can make our teeth decay.

Practice

A. Fill in the missing words to complete the sentences.

| tearing | plaque | digested | bacteria | grinding | decay |

1. We use our teeth for biting and chewing our food so it can be _____.

2. We clean our teeth to brush away _____.

3. _____ break food down into plaque in our mouths.

4. If we do not brush away plaque our teeth can _____.

5. Animals who do not eat meat need teeth designed for _____ tough plants such as grass and leaves.

6. Animals who only eat meat need teeth for killing prey and _____ chunks of meat.

Extension

B. True or false? Put T or F in the boxes.

1. Eating too many sticky sweets is good for our teeth. ☐
2. Plaque coats our teeth and protects them. ☐
3. We should never brush our teeth in case we wear them away. ☐
4. We need to brush our teeth twice a day. ☐
5. Brushing regularly causes tooth decay. ☐
6. We should visit the dentist once every seven years. ☐

Challenge

C. Look at the picture below. It shows the different types of teeth that humans have.

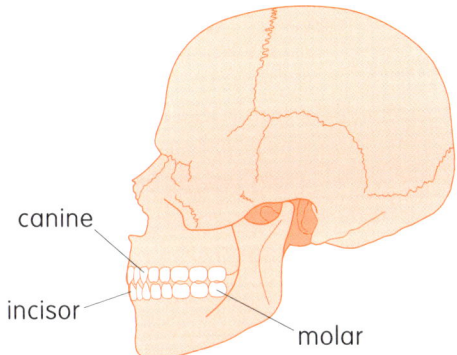

Match the names of the teeth to the job they do.

1. These teeth are sharp and pointed. They are used for tearing food.

2. These teeth are large, wide and flat. They have ridges for chewing and grinding food.

3. These teeth are large. They are used for chopping food.

a. incisors

b. molars

c. canines

TOPIC 10: Muscles and bones

Focus

We have bones for three reasons:

- To give our bodies support.
- To protect the important soft parts or **organs** inside our bodies – such as our brain, lungs and heart.
- To help us to move about. Our muscles work with our bones to help us walk, run, bend and carry things.

We call the place where two bones join a **joint**. Our elbows and knees are examples of joints.

Practice

A. Fill in the missing words from the box below to complete the sentences.

support	bones	joints	muscles	move	organs	lungs	skull

1. _____ help to protect the organs inside our bodies.

2. Your bones, together with your _____, help you to move about.

3. Bones _____ your body, allowing you to stand up instead of flopping about.

4. Your knees and your elbows are examples of _____.

5. Without bones and muscles, people would not be able to _____ about.

6. Your ribs protect soft _____ like your heart.

7. Your _____ protects your brain.

8. Our _____ are protected by our rib cages.

Extension

B. Match the name of the bone to the job it does.

1. Protect our lungs, heart and other soft parts inside our chests.

2. Helps us to stand up straight, and also bend over.

3. Protects our brain.

a. skull

b. ribs

c. backbone

Challenge

C. Label this skeleton, using the words in the boxes.

| elbow joint | skull | backbone | ribs | knee joint |

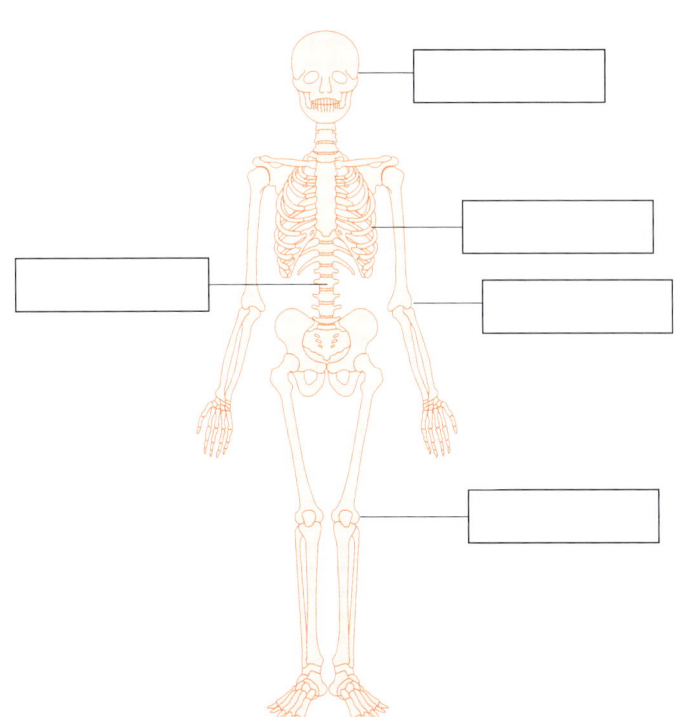

TOPIC 11: **Nutrition**

Focus

We need to eat lots of different types of food to keep healthy. Varied meals of several different foods give us all the food groups and **nutrients** we need.

Fresh fruit and vegetables contain **fibre** and **vitamins**. Wheat cereals and wholemeal bread also contain a lot of fibre.

Butter and cooking oils are **fats**, which provide us with storable energy. We do not need too much of these.

Pasta, cereal and bread contain **carbohydrates**, which give us easy-to-use energy. Runners and athletes often eat pasta meals before a competition.

Cheese, meat, fish, milk and nuts contain **protein**, which helps our bodies to grow and repair themselves.

Dairy products such as cheese, milk and yoghurt contain **calcium**, which we need to build healthy bones and teeth.

Practice

A. Why do we need these foods to stay healthy? Match the name of the food to the job it does.

1. protein – cheese, milk, fish, meat

2. fats – oils and butter

3. carbohydrates – pasta, bread, cereal

4. dairy products

a. give us easy-to-use energy

b. help to build healthy bones and teeth

c. helps our bodies to grow and repair themselves

d. provide storable energy

Extension

B. Which meal is the healthier option? Tick the correct box.

1. a. cheese salad sandwich with wholemeal bread + glass of apple juice .... ☐
   or
   b. cheese pasty and chips + glass of fizzy lemonade .... ☐

2. a. beans on toast + glass of milk .... ☐
   or
   b. pizza + limeade .... ☐

3. a. burger and chips + cola .... ☐
   or
   b. vegetable soup with a wholemeal roll + orange juice .... ☐

Challenge

C. Fill in the missing words to complete the sentences. Use the words in the box below.

| calcium | vitamins | protein | wholemeal | butter |

1. Fibre is found in vegetables, cereal and _____ bread.

2. Fresh fruit is a good source of fibre and _____.

3. Cheese, milk and yoghurt are all good sources of _____. We need this to keep our teeth and bones healthy.

4. _____ and cooking oils contain high levels of fat.

5. _____ helps your body to repair itself when you are hurt.

TOPIC 12: The heart and blood

Focus

The **heart** is a big **muscle** that pumps the blood around our body and keeps it moving. The heart pushes the blood through tubes which carry the blood around our bodies. These tubes are called **veins** and **arteries**.

When we do exercise, our heart beats faster. We also breathe more quickly. This is because our bodies need more **oxygen**. Oxygen is dissolved in our blood and carried to all parts of our bodies.

Practice

A. Fill in the missing words to complete the sentences.

arteries	heart	veins	pump	oxygen	muscle	faster	breathe

1. The heart acts like a _____, moving blood around the body.
2. The tubes that carry blood around our bodies are called _____ and arteries.
3. Blood carries _____ around our bodies. It also contains dissolved nutrients from our food.
4. When we exercise, our hearts beat _____.
5. A heart is a big _____.
6. _____ and veins carry blood around our bodies.
7. Our _____ is in our chest.
8. We _____ more quickly when we exercise.

Extension

B. True or false? Put T or F in the boxes.

1. The lungs act like a big windmill, moving air around the body. ☐
2. Veins and arteries are the tubes that move blood around the body. ☐
3. When we exercise, our hearts beat slower. ☐
4. The heart is a big joint, like the elbow. ☐
5. Blood carries pieces of food around the body. ☐
6. Blood carries dissolved nutrients from our food around our bodies. ☐

Challenge

C. Fill in the missing letters in these words from this topic.

1. e x _ _ _ _ s e
2. _ _ s c l e
3. _ _ o _ d
4. v _ _ _ s
5. p _ _ p
6. o _ _ _ e n
7. _ e a _ _
8. _ r _ e _ i _ s

TEST 2

Topic 7

1. **What is a habitat?** (1 mark) _____
   _____

2. **What is an ecosystem?** (1 mark) _____
   _____

Topic 8

3. **Draw arrows to show the direction of energy flow in this food chain.** (2 marks)

   | dandelion | snail | hedgehog |

4. **What would happen to the hedgehogs in this food chain if all the snails died?** (1 mark)
   _____

Topic 9

5. **What is plaque?** (2 marks) _____
   _____

6. **How can we keep our teeth healthy? Try to think of three ways.** (3 marks) _____
   _____
   _____
   _____

Topic 10

7. Why do humans have bones? Give two reasons. (2 marks) _____

_____   _____

8. Which bones protect the organs inside the chest (such as the heart and lungs)? (1 mark)

_____

Topic 11

9. Match the food to the food group. (3 marks)

1. pasta	a. protein
2. butter	b. fat
3. fish	c. carbohydrate

10. Choose the best word to complete the sentence. (1 mark)

Milk contains calcium/carbohydrates/fat, which we need to build healthy bones and teeth.

Topic 12

11. Choose the best words to complete the sentences. (2 marks)

a. The heart acts like a machine/pump/container.

b. When we exercise, our hearts beat slower/at the same rate/faster.

Mark the test. Remember to fill in your score on page 3.

Write your score out of 19. ☐

Add a BONUS POINT if you scored 15 or more.

TOTAL SCORE FOR TEST 2 ☐

How did you find the test?
Colour a face

too hard   too easy   about right

TOPIC 13: Healthy living

Focus

To stay healthy, people need to do some exercise, eat the right foods, including fresh fruit and vegetables, and get enough sleep. People should also drink plenty of water each day – around eight glasses for an average-sized adult.

Too much sugar or fat in a person's diet can cause them to become overweight (fat and unfit).

Smoking tobacco, in the form of cigarettes, is bad for the health. It can cause cancer and breathing problems. Breathing in other people's smoke is called "passive smoking". This is also unhealthy.

Too much alcohol, like wine and beer, can also harm people's health.

Practice

A. True or false? Put T or F in the boxes.

1. Smoking is good for you. ....
2. Sugar is good for your teeth. ....
3. Adults should drink lots of alcohol as it is good for their health. ....
4. You should eat as much sugar as possible to give you lots of energy. ....
5. Fresh fruit and vegetables should not be eaten every day. ....
6. We need to drink lots of water to keep ourselves healthy. ....
7. Passive smoking is not harmful. ....
8. Getting enough sleep is important to stay healthy. ....

Extension

B. Answer these.

1. What should people do to keep themselves healthy? _____
   _____
   _____

2. Why is smoking unhealthy? _____
   _____

3. What is meant by "passive smoking"? _____

4. How much water should an average adult drink each day in order to stay healthy?
   _____

5. Eating too much sugar can be bad for you. Give two reasons why. _____
   _____
   _____

Challenge

C. Draw a design for a poster in the box below, telling people how to stay healthy. You could talk about smoking, alcohol, diet and exercise.

TOPIC 14: Natural and synthetic materials

Focus

A **material** is what an object is made from. Wood, metal, plastic, glass, stone, fabric – these are all materials. Some materials, such as plastic, are **synthetic**. This means that they have been made by people. **Natural** materials are those that are found "in nature", such as stone and wool.

Practice

A. Natural or synthetic? Put these items into the correct part of the table.

| leather   chalk   wood   plastic   sand   glass   oil   paper |

natural	synthetic

Extension

B. Match the object to the natural material it is made from.

1. jumper
2. newspaper
3. duvet filling
4. statue

a. stone
b. wool
c. wood
d. feathers

Challenge

C. Look at each of the natural materials shown below. Make a list of the things they can be made into.

1. wool from sheep: _____

2. wood from trees: _____

3. feathers from birds: _____

4. rubber from rubber tree sap: _____

5. stone: _____

TOPIC 15: Solids, liquids and gases

Focus

Materials can be sorted into three groups: **solid**, **liquid** or **gas**.

Liquids flow and change shape to "fit" the container they are held in. Think of the way water can be poured from a jug into a glass.

Solids do not flow or change shape in the same way. Think of a stone, lying on the ground.

Gases also flow and change shape, but they spread out to completely "fill" a space – even a space as big as a room. Think of the way smoke spreads out above a bonfire.

Practice

A. Solid, liquid or gas? You choose! Write the names of the materials in the correct shape.

oxygen	water	clear soup	cola
	glass	steam	carbon dioxide	
air	stone	rigid plastic	polystyrene

solid

liquid

gas

Extension

B. Complete the sentences using the words solid**,** liquid **or** gas**.**

1. Coal is a _____.
2. Blood is a thick _____.
3. The oxygen that divers breathe from tanks underwater is a _____.
4. Party balloons that float are often filled with the _____ helium.
5. Hot air balloons are filled with a _____.
6. Water is a transparent, colourless _____.
7. Ice is a _____ until it melts!

Challenge

C. Materials can sometimes be changed from one state (solid, liquid, gas) to another. Fill in the boxes below to show what state the material is in at each stage.

1. Water [_____] is boiled and becomes steam [_____].

2. Snow [_____] melts in the sunlight and turns back into water [_____].

3. An ice lolly [_____] falls on the floor on a sunny day. It melts [_____].

4. Steam [_____] hits a mirror and cools. It runs down as condensation [_____].

5. An egg [_____] is broken into a pan. It is cooked [_____].

TOPIC 16: Mixtures and filtration

Focus

When tea leaves (solid) are mixed with water (liquid), we have made a **mixture**. We can separate the two materials we have mixed by a process called **filtration**. This means the solid is "sieved" out of the liquid. When we make a cup of tea with tea leaves, we pour the tea out through a strainer.

In science, we usually use **filter paper** for filtration. A mixture is poured through the paper, and the liquid runs through. The solid is caught in the paper.

Practice

A. Which of these mixtures could you separate using filtration?

Put a tick or a cross in the boxes.

Be careful – it is tricky!

1. twigs and pebbles in water .... ☐

2. sugar in hot water .... ☐

3. sugar in cold water .... ☐

4. salt in cold water .... ☐

5. salt in hot water .... ☐

6. sand in water .... ☐

7. gravel in hot water .... ☐

8. instant coffee granules in water .... ☐

Extension

B. Which of these actions involve filtration? Put a tick or a cross in the boxes.

1. Making a cup of tea using tea leaves. .... ☐

2. Cleaning leaves out of a paddling pool using a net. .... ☐

3. Warming soup. .... ☐

4. Draining sweetcorn for dinner in a colander. .... ☐

5. Leaving a bowl of sugary water on the windowsill so the water evaporates. .... ☐

6. Pouring coffee made with instant coffee granules into a cup. .... ☐

Challenge

C. Using the following equipment, draw a diagram to show how you would separate sand from water by filtration.

TOPIC 17: Dissolving and evaporating

Focus

When a solid can be mixed with a liquid, and the solid seems to disappear and actually combines with the liquid, we say it has **dissolved**. When you add sugar to hot tea, the sugar seems to disappear. As you stir the tea, at first you can hear the sugar grating against the edge of the cup. As you keep stirring, the sound gradually disappears. The sugar has dissolved in the water.

You cannot separate a dissolved solid from the liquid in which it is dissolved by filtration. Instead, the liquid must be heated until it boils off, leaving the solid behind. This process is called **evaporation**.

Practice

A. Which of these materials would you separate using evaporation?

Careful – it is trickier than it looks. Some things could be separated by evaporation, but it might be easier to use filtration. Tick the box if you would use evaporation, or put a cross if you would not.

1. twigs and pebbles in water .... ☐

2. sugar in hot water .... ☐

3. sugar in cold water .... ☐

4. salt in cold water .... ☐

5. salt in hot water .... ☐

6. sand in water .... ☐

7. gravel in hot water .... ☐

8. instant coffee granules in water .... ☐

Extension

B. Which of these actions involve evaporation? Put a tick in the correct boxes.

1. Making a cup of tea using tea leaves. ☐

2. Cleaning leaves out of a paddling pool using a net. ☐

3. Separating salt from seawater to make fresh water. ☐

4. Draining the water from a pan of potatoes for dinner in a colander. ☐

5. Leaving a bowl of sugary water on the windowsill so the water disappears and crystals are left. ☐

Challenge

C. Using the following equipment and anything else you would need, draw a diagram to show how you would separate salt from water by evaporation.

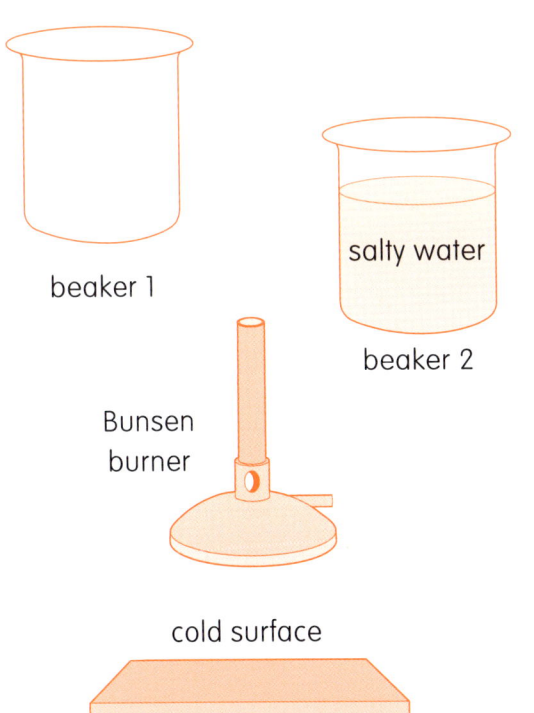

beaker 1

salty water

beaker 2

Bunsen burner

cold surface

TOPIC 18: **Sound**

Focus

Sound travels in invisible **waves** through the air. We hear things as the sound waves enter our ears. The sound waves make our eardrums vibrate, and tiny bones move inside our ears. We "hear" the vibration as "sound".

The loudness of sound is measured in **decibels** (dB).

The closer we are to the thing making the noise, the louder we hear the sound. Very loud sounds can be dangerous as they can damage our ears. This is why we see people wearing ear protectors when they are working with loud tools such as pneumatic drills. Hearing can also be affected by illnesses and infections, but doctors can usually treat these problems.

Practice

A. Answer these.

1. What unit is the loudness of sound measured in? _____

2. Does a noise sound louder closer to or further away from the thing making the noise? _____

3. Why do people using machinery wear special ear protectors? _____
   _____

4. How does sound travel through the air? _____

5. Why are loud sounds bad for your ears? _____
   _____

6. What noisy environments might damage your ears? _____
   _____
   _____

Extension

B. True or false? Put T or F in the boxes.

1. You should never poke anything in your ear, in case you cause damage. ....☐
2. The further away you are from a noise, the louder it is. ....☐
3. People wear ear protectors to make noises sound louder. ....☐
4. Loud noises can damage the ears. ....☐
5. We hear things as sound enters our noses. ....☐
6. Hearing can be affected by infections such as colds and flu. ....☐

Challenge

C. Look at the picture below. Where would the number of decibels of sound from the radio be greatest? Circle A, B or C.

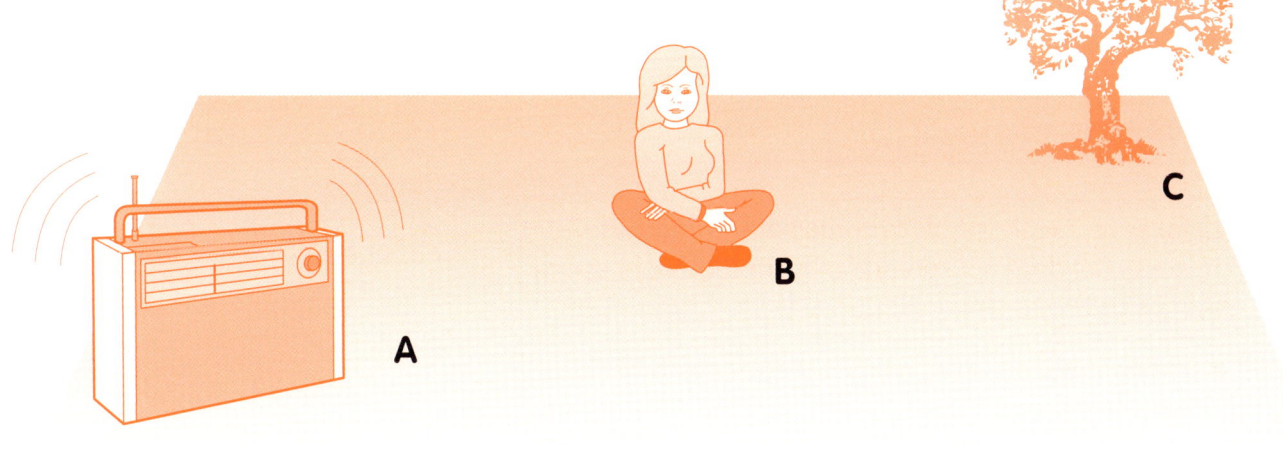

Give a reason for your answer. _____

_____

_____

TEST 3

Topic 13

1. **What is "passive smoking"?** (1 mark) _____
   _____

2. **About how many glasses of water should an adult drink a day?** (1 mark) _____

Topic 14

3. **If we say that a material is "synthetic", what does this mean?** (1 mark) _____
   _____

Topic 15

4. **Match the description to the material.** (3 marks)

   | 1. keeps its shape, does not flow, does not spread out to take up more space | **a.** milk – a liquid |

   | 2. takes on the shape of the container it is in, flows easily but does not spread out to take up more space | **b.** air – a gas |

   | 3. changes shape, flows easily, spreads out to fill whatever space it is in | **c.** wood – a solid |

5. **Imagine you are holding a plastic beaker of fizzy cola. Give the answer** solid, liquid **or** gas. (3 marks)

   a. What is the plastic beaker? _____

   b. What is the cola? _____

   c. What are the bubbles? _____

Topic 16

6. **What process would you use to separate gravel from water?** (1 mark) _____

7. **What process would you use to separate sugar from water?** (1 mark) _____

8. **Which of these actions involve filtration? Tick the correct boxes.** (2 marks)
   a. Making a cup of tea using tea leaves. .... ☐
   b. Cleaning leaves out of a paddling pool using a net. .... ☐
   c. Leaving a bowl of salty water on the windowsill so the water disappears. .... ☐
   d. Pouring coffee made with instant coffee granules into a cup. .... ☐

Topic 17

9. **Which of the following materials will dissolve in water? Circle them.** (2 marks)

   sand   gravel   salt   sugar   glitter

10. **Choose the best word to complete the sentence.** (1 mark)

    When washing is drying, the process taking place is called contamination/condensation/evaporation.

Topic 18

11. **Fill in the blanks.** (3 marks)

    Sound travels in invisible _____ through the air. The sound waves make our _____ vibrate, and tiny _____ move inside our ears. We "hear" the vibration as "sound".

Mark the test. Remember to fill in your score on page 3.

Write your score out of 19. ☐

Add a BONUS POINT if you scored 15 or more.

TOTAL SCORE FOR TEST 3 ☐

How did you find the test?
Colour a face

too hard   too easy   about right

TOPIC 19: The Earth, the Sun and the Moon

Focus

Do you know why we have seasons? Or why we have day and night? It is all to do with the movement of the Earth in space.

The Earth **orbits** (moves around) the Sun once every 365.25 days – the "0.25" of a day is why we have a "leap year", with an extra day – 29th February – every four years. The Earth also spins once every 24 hours. This is one "day" – a day and a night.

The seasons are caused because the Earth is **tilted** as it moves. When the tilt of the north of the Earth is towards the Sun, we in the north experience spring and summer. When the tilt of the north is away from the Sun, we experience autumn and winter.

Have you ever noticed how the Moon seems to change shape during the course of a month? Sometimes it looks big and round; sometimes it is a banana shape. This is due to the changing position of the Moon as it orbits the Earth every 28 days. The Moon really stays the same shape, but at different times we see it as a changing shape because of the way light from the Sun reflects back off the Moon. (Remember, the Moon does not actually produce any light; it shines with reflected light.)

Practice

A. Fill in the missing words to complete the sentences. Use the words in the box below.

| leap | Earth | tilted | orbits | produce |

1. We have seasons because the spinning Earth is _____ as it moves around the Sun.

2. Every fourth year, we have a _____ year.

3. The _____ moves round the Sun once every 365.25 days.

4. The Moon does not _____ light.

5. The Moon seems to change shape because of its changing position as it _____ the Earth.

Extension

B. True or false? Put T or F in the boxes.

1. The Moon changes shape during the course of the month. ☐
2. The Moon seems to change shape during the course of the month. ☐
3. The Moon does not shine. It reflects light from the Sun. ☐
4. The Moon produces very bright light. ☐
5. The Earth moves around the Sun once every 365.25 days. ☐
6. The Moon moves around the Earth once every 28 days. ☐

Challenge

C. Choose the numbers from the box below to fill the gaps.

| 1 | 28 | 24 | 52 | 4 | 365.25 |

1. There are ☐ hours in a day.
2. We have a leap year every ☐ years.
3. The Earth turns ☐ time in 24 hours.
4. The Moon revolves around the Earth roughly once every ☐ days.
5. There are ☐ weeks in a year.
6. The Earth moves around the Sun once every ☐ days.

TOPIC 20: Reversible and irreversible changes

Focus

We can change the state of materials by heating and cooling.

Some of these changes can be reversed and the material changed back to its original state. Think of an ice lolly (solid) that melts in the warmth of the Sun. It goes runny, changing from a solid to a liquid. It started out as a liquid which was put into a freezer and cooled until it froze and became a solid. We call this a **reversible change** because we have changed the material back into its original state.

Other changes cannot be reversed. This means we change the state of a material and are then unable to change it back. An example would be an egg that had been fried. Before the inside of an egg is cooked, it is a liquid. Once it is fried, it changes state into a solid. It cannot be changed back, so it is an **irreversible change**.

Practice

A. Which of these changes are reversible? Mark the reversible changes with an R.

1. Chocolate melting, changing from a solid to a liquid. ☐

2. Ice melting, changing from a solid to a liquid. ☐

3. Egg cooking, changing from a liquid to a solid. ☐

4. Butter melting, changing from a solid to a liquid. ☐

5. Water boiling, changing from a liquid to a gas. ☐

6. Water freezing, changing from a liquid to a solid. ☐

7. Pancake batter cooking, changing from a liquid to a solid. ☐

Extension

B. How could you reverse these changes of state? By heating or by cooling?
Put H or C in the boxes.

1. Chocolate melting, changing from a solid to a liquid. .... ☐

2. Ice melting, changing from a solid to a liquid. .... ☐

3. Butter melting, changing from a solid to a liquid. .... ☐

4. Water boiling, changing from a liquid to a gas. .... ☐

5. Water freezing, changing from a liquid to a solid. .... ☐

Challenge

C. Fill in the missing words – write reversible or irreversible.

1. I fried an egg. The change was _____.

2. I burned some paper. The change was _____.

3. I melted some ice cubes. The change was _____.

4. I boiled some water and filled the kitchen with steam! The change was _____.

5. I left some chocolate on a sunny windowsill and it melted. The change was _____.

6. I baked a cake. The change was _____.

7. I burned some coal on a fire. The change was _____.

8. I made some ice cubes. The change was _____.

TOPIC 21: **Forces**

Focus

There are many types of **forces**. Forces can make things move – or stop them moving!

Gravity is a force. It is the force of gravity that makes things fall when they are dropped. The gravitational pull of the Earth makes this happen. The gravitational pull of the Earth is strong because the Earth is so big.

Friction is also a force. It slows things down, and can stop things from starting to move. It is friction between our shoes and the floor that stops us slipping over. When the floor is wet, friction is reduced and we are more likely to slip. Shoes with "wavy" rubber soles help us to grip – they increase the friction.

Air resistance slows things down too. Racing cars and planes that are designed to go very fast are often pointed at the front end to cut down on air resistance. A flat front end would give a large surface for the air to push back against, creating drag, and it would be more difficult for the car to travel at high speeds.

Practice

A. Answer these.

1. What is the name of the force that makes things fall when they are dropped? _____

2. Why is the gravitational pull of the Earth so great? _____
_____

3. Which force helps to stop us from slipping over? _____

4. Why are we more likely to slip when it is icy? _____
_____

5. Why does a racing car have much less air resistance than a double-decker bus? _____
_____
_____

Extension

B. In which situation would there be less friction? Circle a or b.

1.   **a.** an ice cube being pushed along a smooth table
   or **b.** an ice cube being pushed along a rough concrete path
2.   **a.** someone in a pair of trainers walking on a polished floor
   or **b.** someone in a pair of socks walking on a polished floor
3.   **a.** a sledge moving on a snow-covered hill
   or **b.** a sledge moving on a grassy hill
4.   **a.** an eraser being pushed across a desk
   or **b.** a smooth, flat pencil sharpener being pushed across a desk
5.   **a.** a toy being pushed along a polished floor
   or **b.** a toy being pushed along a rough concrete path
6.   **a.** a cat sliding across a wet floor
   or **b.** a cat sliding across a dry floor

Challenge

C. Draw an aeroplane in the box below. Label the features that will help it to travel fast.

TOPIC 22: Light and how we see things

Focus

Light enables us to see things. We see when light enters our eyes. If things do not give off their own light, we see them when light bounces off them and enters our eyes. Light only travels in straight lines – it cannot bend round things. Shadows are formed when light hits something **opaque** and cannot travel through.

Practice

A. Light travels from a source. That means something that makes its own light.

Look at the objects in the word wall below. Circle all the things that are a source of light.

torch	mirror	lamp	shiny pond
streetlight	TV screen (on)	fire	candle flame
glass	shiny tin foil	firework	shiny spoon
glitter	sequins	digital clock display	cellophane
traffic lights	eye	glass jar	copper pan
cat's eye on road	Moon	lighthouse	red bike reflector

Extension

B. Transparent or opaque? We can see through transparent objects because light can pass through transparent things. Light cannot pass through opaque things. Sort these objects into the boxes.

	opaque	transparent
water		
orange juice		
wood		
glass		
clear plastic		
magazine		
T-shirt		
metal cake tin		

Challenge

C. Look at the picture below. Draw direction arrows on the beam of light to show how the boy can see the butterfly.

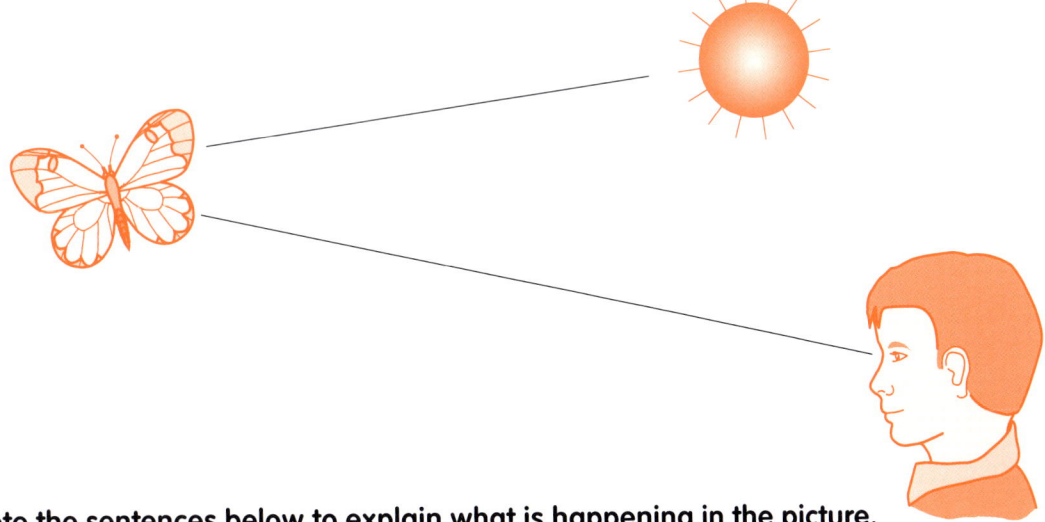

Complete the sentences below to explain what is happening in the picture.

1. The light travels from the _____ to the butterfly.
2. The light bounces off the butterfly and enters the boy's _____.

TOPIC 23: **Magnets**

Focus

Magnets attract metals containing iron, such as steel.

The two ends of a magnet are called **poles**: the north pole and the south pole. If you put two poles that are the same together (north + north or south + south), the magnets will push away from or "repel" each other. We call this **repulsion**. If you put two opposite poles together (north + south), the magnets will be pulled towards each other. We call this **attraction**.

Practice

A. Which objects in the word wall below will be attracted to a magnet? Circle them.

aluminium foil sweet wrapper	steel paper clip	pebble
plastic toy	steel pins	
iron nail	marble	iron filings
wooden lolly stick	gold necklace	

Extension

B. Look at the pairs of bar magnets. Write attract or repel in the boxes to show what will happen.

1. [N|S] [S|N] ⟶ [attract]

2. [S|N] [S|N] ⟶ [repel]

3. [S|N] [N|S] ⟶ [attract]

4. [N|S] [N|S] ⟶ [repel]

C. When you put two "like" poles together (two that are the same), what happens?

_____

Challenge

D. True or false? Put T or F in the boxes.

1. If you put "like" poles together, they will repel each other. ☐

2. If you put opposite poles together, they will repel each other. ☐

3. If you put "like" poles together, they will be attracted to each other. ☐

4. All non-metals are attracted to a magnet. ☐

5. Metals containing iron are attracted to a magnet. ☐

6. If you put two north poles together, they will be attracted to each other. ☐

TOPIC 24: **Electricity**

Focus

We use electricity every day – for lighting, heating, cooking, to run TVs and computers.

Many objects use **mains electricity** – this is the electricity that we can get by putting a plug into a wall socket. It can be dangerous, so NEVER poke anything into a socket or use plugs and switches with wet hands, because you could get an electric shock.

Battery-powered electricity is used in many toys and portable things like radios – this is perfectly safe and is the type of electricity you use in school. Batteries create electricity when the chemicals inside the battery react with each other. NEVER try to open, break or burn a battery because the chemicals can harm your skin.

Car batteries are different. They can be very dangerous as they are powerful and can give you an electric shock. NEVER touch them.

Practice

A. Draw arrows to show which of these objects use mains electricity and which use batteries.

| light bulb in a ceiling fitting | remote-controlled toy car | handheld games console |

mains electricity   batteries

| torch | streetlight | remote-controlled robot | full-size car |

Extension

B. Have you ever made electrical circuits at school? What "jobs" do these circuit components (parts) do when they are connected into a circuit? Match the descriptions to the component names.

pushes the electricity through the wires		wire		used to break the flow of electricity, to turn the bulb on and off
	switch			
gives off light when electricity passes through it		battery		
	bulb			links together different components (parts) in a circuit
makes a noise when electricity passes through it		buzzer		

Challenge

C. Look at the drawing below. Then draw a circuit diagram to represent the drawing, using the symbols given in the box below.

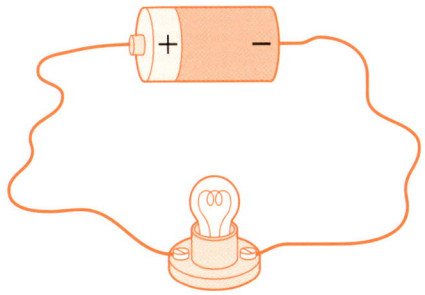

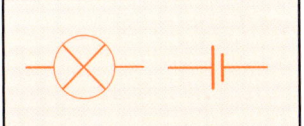

TEST 4

Topic 19

1. **Choose words from the box to fill in the blanks below.** (2 marks)

   | autumn spring summer winter |

   As the north of the Earth tilts towards the Sun, we in the north experience _____ and _____.

   As the north tilts away from the Sun, we experience _____ and _____.

Topic 20

2. **Which of these changes are reversible? Tick them.** (2 marks)

   a. melting chocolate .... ☐

   b. melting an ice cube .... ☐

   c. frying an egg .... ☐

3. **How could you reverse these changes of state? By heating or by cooling?** (2 marks)

   a. Chocolate melting, changing from a solid to a liquid. _____

   b. Ice melting, changing from a solid to a liquid. _____

   c. Butter melting, changing from a solid to a liquid. _____

   d. Water boiling, changing from a liquid to a gas. _____

Topic 21

4. **If I were driving a fast car on a gritty road, which forces would slow me down?** (2 marks) _____

   _____

58

Topic 22

5. **Which of these items are sources of light? Circle them.** (2 marks)

   Sun   Moon   torch   mirror   candle

6. **Match the words to the correct meanings.** (2 marks)

1. "See through" – light can travel through easily. An example would be clear glass.	a. opaque
2. No light can pass through – an example would be cardboard.	b. transparent

Topic 23

7. **True or false? Put T or F in the boxes.** (2 marks)
   a. All non-metals are magnetic. ☐
   b. Metals containing copper are magnetic. ☐
   c. Opposite poles repel. ☐
   d. Opposite poles attract. ☐

8. **Which of these metals would be attracted to a magnet?** (1 mark)
   a. copper
   b. steel
   c. gold

9. **What would happen if you put opposite poles of two magnets together?** (1 mark)

   _____

Topic 24

10. **Name the symbols below used in circuit diagrams.** (3 marks)

    a. 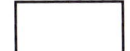 _____   b.  _____   c.  _____

Mark the test. Remember to fill in your score on page 3.

Write your score out of 19. ☐

Add a BONUS POINT if you scored 15 or more.

TOTAL SCORE FOR TEST 4 ☐

How did you find the test?
Colour a face

too hard   too easy   about right

Answers

TOPIC 1: **Parts of a plant and their functions** (page 4)

A.

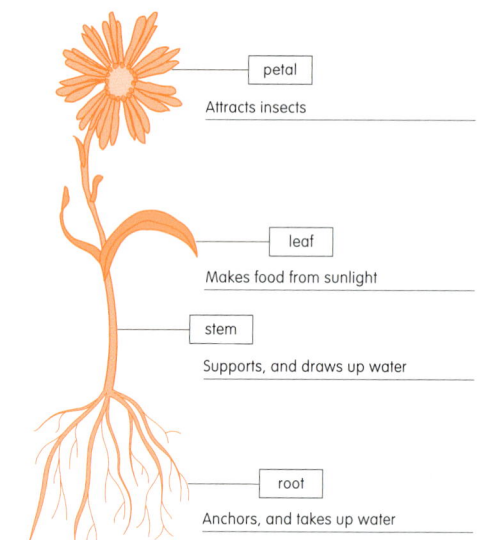

- petal — Attracts insects
- leaf — Makes food from sunlight
- stem — Supports, and draws up water
- root — Anchors, and takes up water

B.
1. b
2. a
3. c
4. d

C.
1. root
2. seeds
3. Sun
4. pollen
5. light

TOPIC 2: **Pollination** (page 6)

A.
1. wind
2. insect
3. insect
4. wind
5. insect
6. wind
7. insect
8. insect

B.
1. ✓   3. ✓   5. ✓

C.
Picture and description of a plant with scent, colour and nectar as features.

TOPIC 3: **Healthy plants** (page 8)

A.
1. c   2. a   3. b

B.
The radiator will dry the compost out, and once the seeds germinate they will be spindly and yellowed due to a lack of light.

C.
1. F   5. T
2. F   6. F
3. F   7. T
4. T   8. T

D.
1. C   2. B   3. A

TOPIC 4: **Micro-organisms** (page 10)

A.
1. mouldy
2. yoghurt
3. micro-organism
4. viruses
5. Bacteria
6. Beer
7. yeast
8. rot

B.
1. d   4. c
2. e   5. a
3. b

C.
1. bread
2. bacteria
3. compost
4. sick
5. Viruses

TOPIC 5: **Sorting and classifying** (page 12)

A.
Lives in water: whale, tadpole, newt, shark
Does not live in water: lion, dog, donkey

B.
Lays eggs: alligator, chicken, penguin, python
Does not lay eggs: whale, dog, donkey

C.
Can fly: bird
Can fly and has 6 legs: butterfly, ladybird, dragonfly, beetle
Has 6 legs: ant
Please note that although some types of ants do fly, the ant shown on page 13 does not have wings, so it cannot fly.

TOPIC 6: **The seven life processes** (page 14)

A.
Alive: cat, spider, beetle
Not alive: pebble, flames, water, sunshine

B.
1. F   4. F
2. F   5. T
3. F   6. T

C.
A mouse does everything on the list so it is alive.
Fire only moves and grows so it is not alive.

TEST 1 (page 16)
Topic 1
1. **1.** c **2.** b **3.** a
2. roots
3. To make food in the leaves.

Topic 2
4. a. ✓ c. ✓ e. ✓

Topic 3
5. light and water
6. It would wilt, go brown and eventually die.
7. It would become spindly and go yellow.

Topic 4
8. To keep it cool so that bacteria do not multiply rapidly.

Topic 5
9. Sorting things into groups according to their characteristics.

Topic 6
10. Alive: tadpole, plant, oak tree
    Not alive: sunshine, water, fire

TOPIC 7: **Habitats and ecosystems** (page 18)
A.
1. d 5. f
2. b 6. e
3. a 7. g
4. c

B.
1. habitat 4. desert
2. seashore 5. ladybirds
3. Woodland

C.
A variety of answers are possible, including:
1. owl, badger, squirrel
2. orchid, tree frog, jaguar
3. limpet, crab, sea anemone
4. cactus, scorpion
5. The place where a collection of plants and animals live.

TOPIC 8: **Food chains** (page 20)
A.
1. seaweed → fish → otter
2. cabbage → snail → hedgehog
3. grass → rabbit → fox
4. plant → caterpillar → robin
5. nuts → mouse → owl

B.
1. caterpillar 4. seagull
2. hedgehog 5. rabbit
3. lettuce

C.
1. cabbage → slug → thrush
2. seeds → mouse → owl
3. pondweed → dragonfly larva → fish

TOPIC 9: **Teeth** (page 22)
A.
1. digested 4. decay
2. plaque 5. grinding
3. Bacteria 6. tearing

B.
1. F 4. T
2. F 5. F
3. F 6. F

C.
1. c 2. b 3. a

TOPIC 10: **Muscles and bones** (page 24)
A.
1. Bones 5. move
2. muscles 6. organs
3. support 7. skull
4. joints 8. lungs

B.
1. b 2. c 3. a

C.
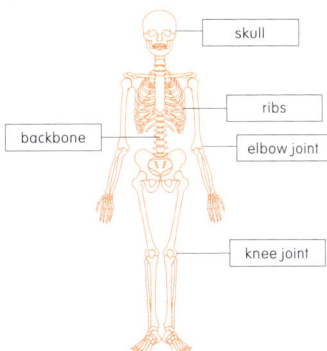

TOPIC 11: **Nutrition** (page 26)
A.
1. c 3. a
2. d 4. b

B.
1. a 2. a 3. b

C.
1. wholemeal
2. vitamins
3. calcium
4. Butter
5. Protein

TOPIC 12: **The heart and blood** (page 28)

A.
1. pump
2. veins
3. oxygen
4. faster
5. muscle
6. Arteries
7. heart
8. breathe

B.
1. F
2. T
3. F
4. F
5. F
6. T

C.
1. exercise
2. muscle
3. blood
4. veins
5. pump
6. oxygen
7. heart
8. arteries

TEST 2 (page 30)

Topic 7
1. A place where certain animals and plants live together.
2. The animals and plants that live together in a habitat make up an ecosystem.

Topic 8
3. dandelion → snail → hedgehog
4. The hedgehogs would starve, find other food or move away to another habitat.

Topic 9
5. Sticky material formed on teeth when bacteria break food down into sugars.
6. Brush teeth twice a day, do not eat lots of sugary foods, visit the dentist twice a year.

Topic 10
7. Any two from support, movement and protection.
8. The ribs.

Topic 11
9. 1. c   2. b   3. a
10. calcium

Topic 12
11. **a.** pump   **b.** faster

TOPIC 13: **Healthy living** (page 32)

A.
1. F
2. F
3. F
4. F
5. F
6. T
7. F
8. T

B.
1. Exercise, eat healthily, sleep well, do not smoke, do not drink too much alcohol.
2. It can cause cancer and breathing problems.
3. Breathing in other people's smoke.
4. Eight glasses a day.
5. It is bad for your teeth and can make you overweight.

C.
Any poster showing the merits of healthy living.

TOPIC 14: **Natural and synthetic materials** (page 34)

A.
Natural: leather, chalk, wood, sand, oil
Synthetic: plastic, glass, paper

B.
1. b
2. c
3. d
4. a

C.
Variety of answers, including:
1. coats, hats, gloves, scarf, loft insulation, blankets, carpets
2. paper, furniture, pencils
3. duvets, pillow fillings
4. rubber bands, rubber matting, tyres, Wellington boots
5. statues, houses, paving slabs

TOPIC 15: **Solids, liquids and gases** (page 36)

A.
Solid: glass, stone, rigid plastic, polystyrene
Liquid: water, clear soup, cola
Gas: oxygen, steam, carbon dioxide, air

B.
1. solid
2. liquid
3. gas
4. gas
5. gas
6. liquid
7. solid

C.
1. liquid, gas
2. solid, liquid
3. solid, liquid
4. gas, liquid
5. liquid, solid

TOPIC 16: **Mixtures and filtration** (page 38)

A.
1. ✓
2. ✗
3. ✗
4. ✗
5. ✗
6. ✓
7. ✓
8. ✗

B.
1. ✓
2. ✓
3. ✗
4. ✓
5. ✗
6. ✗

C.
Diagram showing the water and sand mixture poured into the funnel with the filter paper inside, and the water from the funnel collected in the empty beaker.

TOPIC 17: **Dissolving and evaporating** (page 40)

A.
1. ✗   5. ✓
2. ✓   6. ✗
3. ✓   7. ✗
4. ✓   8. ✓

B.
3. ✓   5. ✓

C.
Diagram illustrating the salty water being heated safely by the Bunsen burner. The cold surface should be above beaker 2 (with the solution) and tilted at an angle so that the condensation runs down into the collecting beaker.

TOPIC 18: **Sound** (page 42)

A.
1. decibels
2. closer to
3. To protect their ears from loud noise.
4. in waves
5. They can hurt them.
6. factories with machinery, rock concerts, etc.

B.
1. T   4. T
2. F   5. F
3. F   6. T

C.
A – it is nearest to the sound being made, so the sound will be loudest here.

TEST 3 (page 44)

Topic 13
1. Breathing in other people's cigarette smoke.
2. eight

Topic 14
3. It is made by people.

Topic 15
4. 1. c   2. a   3. b
5. a. solid
   b. liquid
   c. gas

Topic 16
6. filtration/sieving
7. evaporation
8. a. ✓
   b. ✓

Topic 17
9. salt, sugar
10. evaporation

Topic 18
11. waves, eardrums, bones

TOPIC 19: **The Earth, the Sun and the Moon** (page 46)

A.
1. tilted   4. produce
2. leap   5. orbits
3. Earth

B.
1. F   4. F
2. T   5. T
3. T   6. T

C.
1. 24   4. 28
2. 4   5. 52
3. 1   6. 365.25

TOPIC 20: **Reversible and irreversible changes** (page 48)

A.
Reversible (R): 1, 2, 4, 5, 6

B.
1. C   4. C
2. C   5. H
3. C

C.
1. irreversible   5. reversible
2. irreversible   6. irreversible
3. reversible   7. irreversible
4. reversible   8. reversible

TOPIC 21: **Forces** (page 50)

A.
1. gravity
2. Because the Earth is so large.
3. friction
4. There is less friction.
5. The front of a double-decker bus is large and flat. The front of a racing car is pointed. The car is able to cut through the air more easily than the bus.

B.
1. a   4. b
2. b   5. a
3. a   6. a

C.
Picture of an aeroplane with a sharp, pointy front end and an aerodynamic shape to reduce air resistance.

TOPIC 22: **Light and how we see things** (page 52)

A.
Torch, lamp, streetlight, TV screen (on), fire, candle flame, firework, digital clock display, traffic lights, lighthouse

B.
Opaque: orange juice, wood, magazine, T-shirt, metal cake tin
Transparent: water, glass, clear plastic

C.

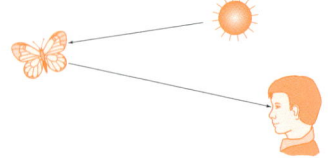

1. Sun   2. eyes

TOPIC 23: **Magnets** (page 54)

A.
steel paper clip, steel pins, iron nail, iron filings

B.
repel, attract, repel, attract

C.
They push apart – repulsion.

D.
1. T   4. F
2. F   5. T
3. F   6. F

TOPIC 24: **Electricity** (page 56)

A.
Mains electricity: light bulb in a ceiling fitting, streetlight
Batteries: remote-controlled toy car, remote-controlled robot, handheld games console, torch, full-size car

B.
bulb – gives off light when electricity passes through it.
wire – links together different components (parts) in a circuit.
switch – used to break the flow of electricity to turn the bulb on and off.
battery – pushes the electricity through the wires.
buzzer – makes a noise when electricity passes through it.

C.

TEST 4 (page 58)

Topic 19
1. spring, summer, autumn, winter

Topic 20
2. a. ✓
   b. ✓
3. a. cooling   c. cooling
   b. cooling   d. cooling

Topic 21
4. friction, air resistance

Topic 22
5. Sun, torch, candle
6. 1. b   2. a

Topic 23
7. a. F   b. F   c. F   d. T
8. b
9. They would attract each other.

Topic 24
10. buzzer, battery (or "cell"), bulb